C000026372

More
Precious
than
Gold

*read the Bible in
one or two years*

ROBERT MURRAY McCHEYNE

The Didasko Files

This growing series takes its name from the New Testament Greek verb *didasko*,
meaning 'I teach'. We trust it will serve the world's Church by helping Christians to
grow in their faith. The series was founded in 2007 by the International Fellowship of
Evangelical Students (IFES), a global movement now in over 150 countries working to
proclaim Christ in the world's universities. www.ifesworld.org

IFES plays an active role in The Lausanne Movement

First published by IFES 2003. Reprinted 2005.

First published by The Lausanne Movement 2008. All rights reserved.

Photographs © IFES. Used with permission.

Designed by Chris Gander
Printed in Singapore by Excel Print Media

'Let the word of Christ dwell in you richly'

God reveals himself to us in Scripture. As we read the Bible daily, he gradually works on our thinking, our will and our emotions so we can love him 'with all our mind, our strength, our soul, our heart'.

This reading plan, drawn up by a Scottish minister, Robert Murray McCheyne (1813-1843) is used by thousands of Christians around the world. It will take you through the New Testament and Psalms twice, and the rest of the Old Testament once, each year. If that is too much to read, you can use it over a two-year cycle by reading two passages instead of four. The readings are set out on separate pages for those who prefer to do this. McCheyne urged Christians to read in more than one part of scripture each day, to get a feel for the whole sweep of salvation history.

The Lausanne Movement has chosen to make the plan widely available to encourage many more Christians to read the whole Bible. If we are to be effective in the work of world evangelization, we must be people whose lives are shaped and strengthened by the Bible. Indeed, it is our supreme authority for what we believe and for how we live.

We all struggle in the daily disciplines of the spiritual life. May this plan help you in your walk with Christ. We join our friends (pp2-3) in commending it to you.

Doug Birdsall
Executive Chairman

Lindsay Brown
International Director

The Lausanne Movement

The late Dr Martyn Lloyd-Jones introduced me to the McCheyne calendar in the 1950s, and I have used it ever since. To me its great value is that it begins with the four 'great beginnings' in Scripture – Genesis (the birth of the universe), Ezra (the rebirth of the nation after Babylonian captivity), Matthew (the birth of Christ) and Acts (the birth of the body of Christ). Then we follow the unfolding of these four stories. Nothing has helped me more than this to grasp the grand themes of the Bible.

John Stott *Honorary Chairman, The Lausanne Movement*

I find that some sections of Scripture which seem to be the least exciting are the ones which speak to areas of greatest need in my spiritual life. So I need to make sure I regularly read the whole Bible. In this way, 'the whole counsel of God' is able to challenge my mind, which is so prone to straying from God's way of thinking.

Ajith Fernando *Director, Sri Lanka Youth for Christ*

Why not use this with a few friends? You can talk about what you've read and keep one another going! I try to understand what I'm reading much more if I know I'm going to have a conversation about it later.

Elaine Duncan *Chief Executive, Scottish Bible Society*

For those whose lifestyle is organized, this system is a great asset, while for those whose lifestyle is more chaotic, it pulls us back into line. Reading the Bible is a tough discipline, and we all fail at times, but do press on and don't be defeated.

Phillip Jensen *Dean of Sydney*

The world is constantly clamouring for our minds, and this is why I warmly encourage you to make use of the McCheyne Bible Reading Plan. It anchors hearts in the Word of God.

Joni Eareckson Tada *President, Joni and Friends*

Let me tell you of one of the greatest challenges and one of the greatest blessings in my life over the past 40 years. The challenge has been to discipline myself to daily Bible reading. The blessing has been in my life through that discipline. This Bible Reading Plan will help both you and me to continue with this discipline.
Peter Maiden *International Director, Operation Mobilisation*

As I strive to be a follower of Christ I am deeply impressed by the way Jesus himself knew the Scriptures, submitted to their authority in his own life, and referred to them constantly in conversations with others. This is what motivates me to immerse my mind day by day in the broad sweep of Scripture.
Mike Treneer *International President, Navigators*

Somehow we must all get to know the Bible, be familiar with its characters and stories, secure in its doctrines, able to feed on its nourishing truths. There is no shortcut to this. Here is one of the more famous and popular systems used over the years. Embrace it enthusiastically and discover if this is the way God will help you to become what you need to be, a Bible-based Christian.
Terry Virgo *Leader, Newfrontiers Team*

How did the life of a man who died aged 29 have such lasting impact? The answer is found in his passion for Christ – expressed in a hunger for holiness, and a heart for the poor and for those who do not know Christ as Saviour. This was the work of the Holy Spirit and the power of God's Word in his life. Robert Murray McCheyne practised and preached this reading plan. You too will find it more precious than gold.
James Hudson Taylor III, *Former General Director,*
OMF International

◆ ◆ ◆

			✔
1	Genesis 1	Matthew 1	☐
2	Genesis 2	Matthew 2	☐
3	Genesis 3	Matthew 3	☐
4	Genesis 4	Matthew 4	☐
5	Genesis 5	Matthew 5	☐
6	Genesis 6	Matthew 6	☐
7	Genesis 7	Matthew 7	☐
8	Genesis 8	Matthew 8	☐
9	Genesis 9-10	Matthew 9	☐
10	Genesis 11	Matthew 10	☐
11	Genesis 12	Matthew 11	☐
12	Genesis 13	Matthew 12	☐
13	Genesis 14	Matthew 13	☐
14	Genesis 15	Matthew 14	☐
15	Genesis 16	Matthew 15	☐
16	Genesis 17	Matthew 16	☐
17	Genesis 18	Matthew 17	☐
18	Genesis 19	Matthew 18	☐
19	Genesis 20	Matthew 19	☐
20	Genesis 21	Matthew 20	☐
21	Genesis 22	Matthew 21	☐
22	Genesis 23	Matthew 22	☐
23	Genesis 24	Matthew 23	☐
24	Genesis 25	Matthew 24	☐
25	Genesis 26	Matthew 25	☐
26	Genesis 27	Matthew 26	☐
27	Genesis 28	Matthew 27	☐
28	Genesis 29	Matthew 28	☐
29	Genesis 30	Mark 1	☐
30	Genesis 31	Mark 2	☐
31	Genesis 32	Mark 3	☐

Ezra 1	Acts 1	☐
Ezra 2	Acts 2	☐
Ezra 3	Acts 3	☐
Ezra 4	Acts 4	☐
Ezra 5	Acts 5	☐
Ezra 6	Acts 6	☐
Ezra 7	Acts 7	☐
Ezra 8	Acts 8	☐
Ezra 9	Acts 9	☐
Ezra 10	Acts 10	☐
Nehemiah 1	Acts 11	☐
Nehemiah 2	Acts 12	☐
Nehemiah 3	Acts 13	☐
Nehemiah 4	Acts 14	☐
Nehemiah 5	Acts 15	☐
Nehemiah 6	Acts 16	☐
Nehemiah 7	Acts 17	☐
Nehemiah 8	Acts 18	☐
Nehemiah 9	Acts 19	☐
Nehemiah 10	Acts 20	☐
Nehemiah 11	Acts 21	☐
Nehemiah 12	Acts 22	☐
Nehemiah 13	Acts 23	☐
Esther 1	Acts 24	☐
Esther 2	Acts 25	☐
Esther 3	Acts 26	☐
Esther 4	Acts 27	☐
Esther 5	Acts 28	☐
Esther 6	Romans 1	☐
Esther 7	Romans 2	☐
Esther 8	Romans 3	☐

FEBRUARY

			✔
1	Genesis 33	Mark 4	☐
2	Genesis 34	Mark 5	☐
3	Genesis 35-36	Mark 6	☐
4	Genesis 37	Mark 7	☐
5	Genesis 38	Mark 8	☐
6	Genesis 39	Mark 9	☐
7	Genesis 40	Mark 10	☐
8	Genesis 41	Mark 11	☐
9	Genesis 42	Mark 12	☐
10	Genesis 43	Mark 13	☐
11	Genesis 44	Mark 14	☐
12	Genesis 45	Mark 15	☐
13	Genesis 46	Mark 16	☐
14	Genesis 47	Luke 1:1-38	☐
15	Genesis 48	Luke 1:39-80	☐
16	Genesis 49	Luke 2	☐
17	Genesis 50	Luke 3	☐
18	Exodus 1	Luke 4	☐
19	Exodus 2	Luke 5	☐
20	Exodus 3	Luke 6	☐
21	Exodus 4	Luke 7	☐
22	Exodus 5	Luke 8	☐
23	Exodus 6	Luke 9	☐
24	Exodus 7	Luke 10	☐
25	Exodus 8	Luke 11	☐
26	Exodus 9	Luke 12	☐
27	Exodus 10	Luke 13	☐
28	Exodus 11-12:20	Luke 14	☐

			✔
1	Exodus 12:21-51	Luke 15	☐
2	Exodus 13	Luke 16	☐
3	Exodus 14	Luke 17	☐
4	Exodus 15	Luke 18	☐
5	Exodus 16	Luke 19	☐
6	Exodus 17	Luke 20	☐
7	Exodus 18	Luke 21	☐
8	Exodus 19	Luke 22	☐
9	Exodus 20	Luke 23	☐
10	Exodus 21	Luke 24	☐
11	Exodus 22	John 1	☐
12	Exodus 23	John 2	☐
13	Exodus 24	John 3	☐
14	Exodus 25	John 4	☐
15	Exodus 26	John 5	☐
16	Exodus 27	John 6	☐
17	Exodus 28	John 7	☐
18	Exodus 29	John 8	☐
19	Exodus 30	John 9	☐
20	Exodus 31	John 10	☐
21	Exodus 32	John 11	☐
22	Exodus 33	John 12	☐
23	Exodus 34	John 13	☐
24	Exodus 35	John 14	☐
25	Exodus 36	John 15	☐
26	Exodus 37	John 16	☐
27	Exodus 38	John 17	☐
28	Exodus 39	John 18	☐
29	Exodus 40	John 19	☐
30	Leviticus 1	John 20	☐
31	Leviticus 2-3	John 21	☐

APRIL

			✔
1	Leviticus 4	Psalms 1-2	☐
2	Leviticus 5	Psalms 3-4	☐
3	Leviticus 6	Psalms 5-6	☐
4	Leviticus 7	Psalms 7-8	☐
5	Leviticus 8	Psalm 9	☐
6	Leviticus 9	Psalm 10	☐
7	Leviticus 10	Psalms 11-12	☐
8	Leviticus 11-12	Psalms 13-14	☐
9	Leviticus 13	Psalms 15-16	☐
10	Leviticus 14	Psalm 17	☐
11	Leviticus 15	Psalm 18	☐
12	Leviticus 16	Psalm 19	☐
13	Leviticus 17	Psalms 20-21	☐
14	Leviticus 18	Psalm 22	☐
15	Leviticus 19	Psalms 23-24	☐
16	Leviticus 20	Psalm 25	☐
17	Leviticus 21	Psalms 26-27	☐
18	Leviticus 22	Psalms 28-29	☐
19	Leviticus 23	Psalm 30	☐
20	Leviticus 24	Psalm 31	☐
21	Leviticus 25	Psalm 32	☐
22	Leviticus 26	Psalm 33	☐
23	Leviticus 27	Psalm 34	☐
24	Numbers 1	Psalm 35	☐
25	Numbers 2	Psalm 36	☐
26	Numbers 3	Psalm 37	☐
27	Numbers 4	Psalm 38	☐
28	Numbers 5	Psalm 39	☐
29	Numbers 6	Psalms 40-41	☐
30	Numbers 7	Psalms 42-43	☐

			✔
1	Numbers 8	Psalm 44	☐
2	Numbers 9	Psalm 45	☐
3	Numbers 10	Psalms 46-47	☐
4	Numbers 11	Psalm 48	☐
5	Numbers 12-13	Psalm 49	☐
6	Numbers 14	Psalm 50	☐
7	Numbers 15	Psalm 51	☐
8	Numbers 16	Psalms 52-54	☐
9	Numbers 17-18	Psalm 55	☐
10	Numbers 19	Psalms 56-57	☐
11	Numbers 20	Psalm 58-59	☐
12	Numbers 21	Psalms 60-61	☐
13	Numbers 22	Psalms 62-63	☐
14	Numbers 23	Psalms 64-65	☐
15	Numbers 24	Psalms 66-67	☐
16	Numbers 25	Psalm 68	☐
17	Numbers 26	Psalm 69	☐
18	Numbers 27	Psalms 70-71	☐
19	Numbers 28	Psalm 72	☐
20	Numbers 29	Psalm 73	☐
21	Numbers 30	Psalm 74	☐
22	Numbers 31	Psalms 75-76	☐
23	Numbers 32	Psalm 77	☐
24	Numbers 33	Psalm 78:1-39	☐
25	Numbers 34	Psalm 78:40-72	☐
26	Numbers 35	Psalm 79	☐
27	Numbers 36	Psalm 80	☐
28	Deuteronomy 1	Psalms 81-82	☐
29	Deuteronomy 2	Psalms 83-84	☐
30	Deuteronomy 3	Psalm 85	☐
31	Deuteronomy 4	Psalms 86-87	☐

JUNE

			✔
1	Deuteronomy 5	Psalm 88	☐
2	Deuteronomy 6	Psalm 89	☐
3	Deuteronomy 7	Psalm 90	☐
4	Deuteronomy 8	Psalm 91	☐
5	Deuteronomy 9	Psalms 92-93	☐
6	Deuteronomy 10	Psalm 94	☐
7	Deuteronomy 11	Psalms 95-96	☐
8	Deuteronomy 12	Psalms 97-98	☐
9	Deuteronomy 13-14	Psalms 99-101	☐
10	Deuteronomy 15	Psalm 102	☐
11	Deuteronomy 16	Psalm 103	☐
12	Deuteronomy 17	Psalm 104	☐
13	Deuteronomy 18	Psalm 105	☐
14	Deuteronomy 19	Psalm 106	☐
15	Deuteronomy 20	Psalm 107	☐
16	Deuteronomy 21	Psalms 108-109	☐
17	Deuteronomy 22	Psalms 110-111	☐
18	Deuteronomy 23	Psalms 112-113	☐
19	Deuteronomy 24	Psalms 114-115	☐
20	Deuteronomy 25	Psalm 116	☐
21	Deuteronomy 26	Psalms 117-118	☐
22	Deuteronomy 27-28:19	Psalm 119:1-24	☐
23	Deuteronomy 28:20-68	Psalm 119:25-48	☐
24	Deuteronomy 29	Psalm 119:49-72	☐
25	Deuteronomy 30	Psalm 119:73-96	☐
26	Deuteronomy 31	Psalm 119:97-120	☐
27	Deuteronomy 32	Psalm 119:121-144	☐
28	Deuteronomy 33-34	Psalm 119:145-176	☐
29	Joshua 1	Psalms 120-122	☐
30	Joshua 2	Psalms 123-125	☐

JULY

			✔
1	Joshua 3	Psalms 126-128	☐
2	Joshua 4	Psalms 129-131	☐
3	Joshua 5	Psalms 132-134	☐
4	Joshua 6	Psalms 135-136	☐
5	Joshua 7	Psalms 137-138	☐
6	Joshua 8	Psalm 139	☐
7	Joshua 9	Psalms 140-141	☐
8	Joshua 10	Psalms 142-143	☐
9	Joshua 11	Psalm 144	☐
10	Joshua 12-13	Psalm 145	☐
11	Joshua 14-15	Psalms 146-147	☐
12	Joshua 16-17	Psalm 148	☐
13	Joshua 18-19	Psalms 149-150	☐
14	Joshua 20-21	Acts 1	☐
15	Joshua 22	Acts 2	☐
16	Joshua 23	Acts 3	☐
17	Joshua 24	Acts 4	☐
18	Judges 1	Acts 5	☐
19	Judges 2	Acts 6	☐
20	Judges 3	Acts 7	☐
21	Judges 4	Acts 8	☐
22	Judges 5	Acts 9	☐
23	Judges 6	Acts 10	☐
24	Judges 7	Acts 11	☐
25	Judges 8	Acts 12	☐
26	Judges 9	Acts 13	☐
27	Judges 10	Acts 14	☐
28	Judges 11	Acts 15	☐
29	Judges 12	Acts 16	☐
30	Judges 13	Acts 17	☐
31	Judges 14	Acts 18	☐

Isaiah 63	Matthew 11	☐
Isaiah 64	Matthew 12	☐
Isaiah 65	Matthew 13	☐
Isaiah 66	Matthew 14	☐
Jeremiah 1	Matthew 15	☐
Jeremiah 2	Matthew 16	☐
Jeremiah 3	Matthew 17	☐
Jeremiah 4	Matthew 18	☐
Jeremiah 5	Matthew 19	☐
Jeremiah 6	Matthew 20	☐
Jeremiah 7	Matthew 21	☐
Jeremiah 8	Matthew 22	☐
Jeremiah 9	Matthew 23	☐
Jeremiah 10	Matthew 24	☐
Jeremiah 11	Matthew 25	☐
Jeremiah 12	Matthew 26	☐
Jeremiah 13	Matthew 27	☐
Jeremiah 14	Matthew 28	☐
Jeremiah 15	Mark 1	☐
Jeremiah 16	Mark 2	☐
Jeremiah 17	Mark 3	☐
Jeremiah 18	Mark 4	☐
Jeremiah 19	Mark 5	☐
Jeremiah 20	Mark 6	☐
Jeremiah 21	Mark 7	☐
Jeremiah 22	Mark 8	☐
Jeremiah 23	Mark 9	☐
Jeremiah 24	Mark 10	☐
Jeremiah 25	Mark 11	☐
Jeremiah 26	Mark 12	☐
Jeremiah 27	Mark 13	☐

AUGUST

			✔
1	Judges 15	Acts 19	☐
2	Judges 16	Acts 20	☐
3	Judges 17	Acts 21	☐
4	Judges 18	Acts 22	☐
5	Judges 19	Acts 23	☐
6	Judges 20	Acts 24	☐
7	Judges 21	Acts 25	☐
8	Ruth 1	Acts 26	☐
9	Ruth 2	Acts 27	☐
10	Ruth 3-4	Acts 28	☐
11	1 Samuel 1	Romans 1	☐
12	1 Samuel 2	Romans 2	☐
13	1 Samuel 3	Romans 3	☐
14	1 Samuel 4	Romans 4	☐
15	1 Samuel 5-6	Romans 5	☐
16	1 Samuel 7-8	Romans 6	☐
17	1 Samuel 9	Romans 7	☐
18	1 Samuel 10	Romans 8	☐
19	1 Samuel 11	Romans 9	☐
20	1 Samuel 12	Romans 10	☐
21	1 Samuel 13	Romans 11	☐
22	1 Samuel 14	Romans 12	☐
23	1 Samuel 15	Romans 13	☐
24	1 Samuel 16	Romans 14	☐
25	1 Samuel 17	Romans 15	☐
26	1 Samuel 18	Romans 16	☐
27	1 Samuel 19	1 Corinthians 1	☐
28	1 Samuel 20	1 Corinthians 2	☐
29	1 Samuel 21-22	1 Corinthians 3	☐
30	1 Samuel 23	1 Corinthians 4	☐
31	1 Samuel 24	1 Corinthians 5	☐

Jeremiah 28	Mark 14	☐
Jeremiah 29	Mark 15	☐
Jeremiah 30-31	Mark 16	☐
Jeremiah 32	Psalm 1-2	☐
Jeremiah 33	Psalm 3-4	☐
Jeremiah 34	Psalm 5-6	☐
Jeremiah 35	Psalm 7-8	☐
Jeremiah 36	Psalm 9	☐
Jeremiah 37	Psalm 10	☐
Jeremiah 38	Psalm 11-12	☐
Jeremiah 39	Psalm 13-14	☐
Jeremiah 40	Psalm 15-16	☐
Jeremiah 41	Psalm 17	☐
Jeremiah 42	Psalm 18	☐
Jeremiah 43	Psalm 19	☐
Jeremiah 44-45	Psalm 20-21	☐
Jeremiah 46	Psalm 22	☐
Jeremiah 47	Psalm 23-24	☐
Jeremiah 48	Psalm 25	☐
Jeremiah 49	Psalm 26-27	☐
Jeremiah 50	Psalm 28-29	☐
Jeremiah 51	Psalm 30	☐
Jeremiah 52	Psalm 31	☐
Lamentations 1	Psalm 32	☐
Lamentations 2	Psalm 33	☐
Lamentations 3	Psalm 34	☐
Lamentations 4	Psalm 35	☐
Lamentations 5	Psalm 36	☐
Ezekiel 1	Psalm 37	☐
Ezekiel 2	Psalm 38	☐
Ezekiel 3	Psalm 39	☐

SEPTEMBER

			✔
1	1 Samuel 25	1 Corinthians 6	☐
2	1 Samuel 26	1 Corinthians 7	☐
3	1 Samuel 27	1 Corinthians 8	☐
4	1 Samuel 28	1 Corinthians 9	☐
5	1 Samuel 29-30	1 Corinthians 10	☐
6	1 Samuel 31	1 Corinthians 11	☐
7	2 Samuel 1	1 Corinthians 12	☐
8	2 Samuel 2	1 Corinthians 13	☐
9	2 Samuel 3	1 Corinthians 14	☐
10	2 Samuel 4-5	1 Corinthians 15	☐
11	2 Samuel 6	1 Corinthians 16	☐
12	2 Samuel 7	2 Corinthians 1	☐
13	2 Samuel 8-9	2 Corinthians 2	☐
14	2 Samuel 10	2 Corinthians 3	☐
15	2 Samuel 11	2 Corinthians 4	☐
16	2 Samuel 12	2 Corinthians 5	☐
17	2 Samuel 13	2 Corinthians 6	☐
18	2 Samuel 14	2 Corinthians 7	☐
19	2 Samuel 15	2 Corinthians 8	☐
20	2 Samuel 16	2 Corinthians 9	☐
21	2 Samuel 17	2 Corinthians 10	☐
22	2 Samuel 18	2 Corinthians 11	☐
23	2 Samuel 19	2 Corinthians 12	☐
24	2 Samuel 20	2 Corinthians 13	☐
25	2 Samuel 21	Galatians 1	☐
26	2 Samuel 22	Galatians 2	☐
27	2 Samuel 23	Galatians 3	☐
28	2 Samuel 24	Galatians 4	☐
29	1 Kings 1	Galatians 5	☐
30	1 Kings 2	Galatians 6	☐

Ezekiel 4	Psalms 40-41	☐
Ezekiel 5	Psalm 42-43	☐
Ezekiel 6	Psalm 44	☐
Ezekiel 7	Psalm 45	☐
Ezekiel 8	Psalms 46-47	☐
Ezekiel 9	Psalm 48	☐
Ezekiel 10	Psalm 49	☐
Ezekiel 11	Psalm 50	☐
Ezekiel 12	Psalm 51	☐
Ezekiel 13	Psalms 52-54	☐
Ezekiel 14	Psalm 55	☐
Ezekiel 15	Psalms 56-57	☐
Ezekiel 16	Psalm 58-59	☐
Ezekiel 17	Psalm 60-61	☐
Ezekiel 18	Psalm 62-63	☐
Ezekiel 19	Psalm 64-65	☐
Ezekiel 20	Psalm 66-67	☐
Ezekiel 21	Psalm 68	☐
Ezekiel 22	Psalm 69	☐
Ezekiel 23	Psalm 70-71	☐
Ezekiel 24	Psalm 72	☐
Ezekiel 25	Psalm 73	☐
Ezekiel 26	Psalm 74	☐
Ezekiel 27	Psalm 75-76	☐
Ezekiel 28	Psalm 77	☐
Ezekiel 29	Psalm 78:1-39	☐
Ezekiel 30	Psalm 78:40-72	☐
Ezekiel 31	Psalm 79	☐
Ezekiel 32	Psalm 80	☐
Ezekiel 33	Psalm 81-82	☐

OCTOBER

			✔
1	1 Kings 3	Ephesians 1	☐
2	1 Kings 4-5	Ephesians 2	☐
3	1 Kings 6	Ephesians 3	☐
4	1 Kings 7	Ephesians 4	☐
5	1 Kings 8	Ephesians 5	☐
6	1 Kings 9	Ephesians 6	☐
7	1 Kings 10	Philippians 1	☐
8	1 Kings 11	Philippians 2	☐
9	1 Kings 12	Philippians 3	☐
10	1 Kings 13	Philippians 4	☐
11	1 Kings 14	Colossians 1	☐
12	1 Kings 15	Colossians 2	☐
13	1 Kings 16	Colossians 3	☐
14	1 Kings 17	Colossians 4	☐
15	1 Kings 18	1 Thessalonians 1	☐
16	1 Kings 19	1 Thessalonians 2	☐
17	1 Kings 20	1 Thessalonians 3	☐
18	1 Kings 21	1 Thessalonians 4	☐
19	1 Kings 22	1 Thessalonians 5	☐
20	2 Kings 1	2 Thessalonians 1	☐
21	2 Kings 2	2 Thessalonians 2	☐
22	2 Kings 3	2 Thessalonians 3	☐
23	2 Kings 4	1 Timothy 1	☐
24	2 Kings 5	1 Timothy 2	☐
25	2 Kings 6	1 Timothy 3	☐
26	2 Kings 7	1 Timothy 4	☐
27	2 Kings 8	1 Timothy 5	☐
28	2 Kings 9	1 Timothy 6	☐
29	2 Kings 10-11	2 Timothy 1	☐
30	2 Kings 12	2 Timothy 2	☐
31	2 Kings 13	2 Timothy 3	☐

			✔
1	2 Kings 14	2 Timothy 4	☐
2	2 Kings 15	Titus 1	☐
3	2 Kings 16	Titus 2	☐
4	2 Kings 17	Titus 3	☐
5	2 Kings 18	Philemon	☐
6	2 Kings 19	Hebrews 1	☐
7	2 Kings 20	Hebrews 2	☐
8	2 Kings 21	Hebrews 3	☐
9	2 Kings 22	Hebrews 4	☐
10	2 Kings 23	Hebrews 5	☐
11	2 Kings 24	Hebrews 6	☐
12	2 Kings 25	Hebrews 7	☐
13	1 Chronicles 1-2	Hebrews 8	☐
14	1 Chronicles 3-4	Hebrews 9	☐
15	1 Chronicles 5-6	Hebrews 10	☐
16	1 Chronicles 7-8	Hebrews 11	☐
17	1 Chronicles 9-10	Hebrews 12	☐
18	1 Chronicles 11-12	Hebrews 13	☐
19	1 Chronicles 13-14	James 1	☐
20	1 Chronicles 15	James 2	☐
21	1 Chronicles 16	James 3	☐
22	1 Chronicles 17	James 4	☐
23	1 Chronicles 18	James 5	☐
24	1 Chronicles 19-20	1 Peter 1	☐
25	1 Chronicles 21	1 Peter 2	☐
26	1 Chronicles 22	1 Peter 3	☐
27	1 Chronicles 23	1 Peter 4	☐
28	1 Chronicles 24-25	1 Peter 5	☐
29	1 Chronicles 26-27	2 Peter 1	☐
30	1 Chronicles 28	2 Peter 2	☐

Hosea 7	Psalms 120-122	☐
Hosea 8	Psalms 123-125	☐
Hosea 9	Psalms 126-128	☐
Hosea 10	Psalms 129-131	☐
Hosea 11	Psalms 132-134	☐
Hosea 12	Psalms 135-136	☐
Hosea 13	Psalms 137-138	☐
Hosea 14	Psalm 139	☐
Joel 1	Psalms 140-141	☐
Joel 2	Psalm 142	☐
Joel 3	Psalm 143	☐
Amos 1	Psalm 144	☐
Amos 2	Psalm 145	☐
Amos 3	Psalms 146-147	☐
Amos 4	Psalms 148-150	☐
Amos 5	Luke 1:1-38	☐
Amos 6	Luke 1:39-80	☐
Amos 7	Luke 2	☐
Amos 8	Luke 3	☐
Amos 9	Luke 4	☐
Obadiah	Luke 5	☐
Jonah 1	Luke 6	☐
Jonah 2	Luke 7	☐
Jonah 3	Luke 8	☐
Jonah 4	Luke 9	☐
Micah 1	Luke 10	☐
Micah 2	Luke 11	☐
Micah 3	Luke 12	☐
Micah 4	Luke 13	☐
Micah 5	Luke 14	☐

DECEMBER

			✔
1	1 Chronicles 29	2 Peter 3	☐
2	2 Chronicles 1	1 John 1	☐
3	2 Chronicles 2	1 John 2	☐
4	2 Chronicles 3-4	1 John 3	☐
5	2 Chronicles 5-6:11	1 John 4	☐
6	2 Chronicles 6:12-42	1 John 5	☐
7	2 Chronicles 7	2 John	☐
8	2 Chronicles 8	3 John	☐
9	2 Chronicles 9	Jude	☐
10	2 Chronicles 10	Revelation 1	☐
11	2 Chronicles 11-12	Revelation 2	☐
12	2 Chronicles 13	Revelation 3	☐
13	2 Chronicles 14-15	Revelation 4	☐
14	2 Chronicles 16	Revelation 5	☐
15	2 Chronicles 17	Revelation 6	☐
16	2 Chronicles 18	Revelation 7	☐
17	2 Chronicles 19-20	Revelation 8	☐
18	2 Chronicles 21	Revelation 9	☐
19	2 Chronicles 22-23	Revelation 10	☐
20	2 Chronicles 24	Revelation 11	☐
21	2 Chronicles 25	Revelation 12	☐
22	2 Chronicles 26	Revelation 13	☐
23	2 Chronicles 27-28	Revelation 14	☐
24	2 Chronicles 29	Revelation 15	☐
25	2 Chronicles 30	Revelation 16	☐
26	2 Chronicles 31	Revelation 17	☐
27	2 Chronicles 32	Revelation 18	☐
28	2 Chronicles 33	Revelation 19	☐
29	2 Chronicles 34	Revelation 20	☐
30	2 Chronicles 35	Revelation 21	☐
31	2 Chronicles 36	Revelation 22	☐

Micah 6	Luke 15	☐
Micah 7	Luke 16	☐
Nahum 1	Luke 17	☐
Nahum 2	Luke 18	☐
Nahum 3	Luke 19	☐
Habakkuk 1	Luke 20	☐
Habakkuk 2	Luke 21	☐
Habakkuk 3	Luke 22	☐
Zephaniah 1	Luke 23	☐
Zephaniah 2	Luke 24	☐
Zephaniah 3	John 1	☐
Haggai 1	John 2	☐
Haggai 2	John 3	☐
Zechariah 1	John 4	☐
Zechariah 2	John 5	☐
Zechariah 3	John 6	☐
Zechariah 4	John 7	☐
Zechariah 5	John 8	☐
Zechariah 6	John 9	☐
Zechariah 7	John 10	☐
Zechariah 8	John 11	☐
Zechariah 9	John 12	☐
Zechariah 10	John 13	☐
Zechariah 11	John 14	☐
Zechariah 12	John 15	☐
Zechariah 13	John 16	☐
Zechariah 14	John 17	☐
Malachi 1	John 18	☐
Malachi 2	John 19	☐
Malachi 3	John 20	☐
Malachi 4	John 21	☐

The Lausanne Movement

THE WHOLE CHURCH TAKING THE WHOLE GOSPEL TO THE WHOLE WORLD

The Lord Jesus Christ, the eternal Son of God, gave his Church a command which he has never revoked: 'Go and make disciples of all nations.'

'We are,' as the Apostle Paul reminds the Christians in Corinth, 'Christ's ambassadors, as though God were making his appeal through us.'

The Lausanne Movement (also known as the Lausanne Committee on World Evangelization) unites evangelicals around the world in joyful submission to this command and calling. Our desire is to see Christians grow in their knowledge and love of God, and be better equipped to bring the presence of Christ into the professions, academia, family life and society – in all nations. Lausanne has a range of working groups and special interest committees which provide a place for theological and practical discussion, always with the end in view of stimulating more effective evangelism.

The movement, founded by Billy Graham, grew out of a global congress held in Lausanne, Switzerland in 1974. John Stott was the chief architect of the Lausanne Covenant, a major legacy of that congress. This document is widely-regarded as one of the most influential in modern church history. A second congress was held in 1989 in Manila, Philippines, where the Manila Manifesto reaffirmed the call of the Lausanne Covenant to 'Proclaim Christ until he comes'.

For news and reports of Cape Town 2010, The Third Lausanne Congress on World Evangelization, held in partnership with the World Evangelical Alliance, bookmark **www.lausanne.org**

MORE On our website you will find Lausanne's Occasional Papers. You can sign up to receive the monthly *Lausanne Connecting Point* enewsletter and find links to *LausanneWorldPulse.com*, a monthly online missions and evangelism magazine.
www.lausanne.org Email: info@lausanne.org

Also in this series

The Grace of Giving by John Stott

An Authentic Servant by Ajith Fernando

Light, Salt and the World of Business by Fred Catherwood

Further titles in preparation including

Consider the Cross

For the Lord we Love

Didasko File distributors

North America STL Distribution www.stl-distribution.com
Australia and New Zealand Word www.word.com.au
Singapore Armour Publishing www.armourpublishing.com
East Asia (not Singapore) OMF Literature Inc www.omflit.com
Europe 10ofthose.com   www.10ofthose.com
Southern Africa Christian Book Discounters www.christianbooks.co.za
Rest of the world 10ofthose.com www.10ofthose.com

Recommended reading

God's Big Picture by Vaughan Roberts ISBN 978 085 111 2985
How God's plan unfolds from Genesis to Revelation.

For the Love of God by D A Carson ISBN 978 085 111 9748
A daily reflection on one reading from the McCheyne scheme.

The Bible Speaks Today series, covering most Bible books.
For personal study or for preparation to lead a group.

New Bible Commentary ISBN 085 110 648X
Consulting eds: A R Millard, Howard Marshall, J I Packer, D J Wiseman
Includes articles on Bible history and how to approach Scripture.

Travel With Robert Murray McCheyne by Derek Prime
ISBN 978 184625-05-76 A well-illustrated biography.